Eye on the Universe

The Moon

A Bobbie Kalman Book

Niki Walker

Crabtree Publishing Company

Eye on the Universe

Created by Bobbie Kalman

For Greg

Editor-in-Chief
Bobbie Kalman

Written by
Niki Walker

Managing editor
Lynda Hale

Editors
Greg Nickles
Jacqueline Langille
April Fast

Computer design
Lynda Hale
Lucy DeFazio
Campbell Creative Services

Special thanks to
Dr. A. Wesley Ward, Jr., Adrienne Wasserman,
and Don Bills, United States Geological Survey;
Debra L. Dodds, NASA; Elizabeth "Betsy" Carter,
Ames Research Center, NASA

Consultant
Dr. A. Wesley Ward, Jr., Chief,
Astrogeology Program, U.S. Geological Survey,
Flagstaff, Arizona

Production coordinator
Hannelore Sotzek

Printer
Worzalla Publishing Company

Color separations and film
Dot 'n Line Image Inc.

Crabtree Publishing Company

350 Fifth Avenue	360 York Road, RR 4,	73 Lime Walk
Suite 3308	Niagara-on-the-Lake,	Headington
New York	Ontario, Canada	Oxford OX3 7AD
N.Y. 10118	L0S 1J0	United Kingdom

Cataloging in Publication Data
Walker, Niki
 The Moon

(Eye on the universe)
Includes index.

ISBN 0-86505-679-X (library bound) ISBN 0-86505-689-7 (pbk.)
This book describes the characteristics of the Moon and traces the history
of human exploration of Earth's nearest neighbor.

1. Moon—Juvenile literature. [1. Moon.] I. Title. II. Series: Kalman, Bobbie.
Eye on the universe.

QB582.W25 1998   j523.3   LC 98-12997
                                            CIP

Contents

Meet the Moon   4

How the Moon was "born"   6

What is it like on the Moon?   8

The lunar landscape   10

Craters and maria   12

The Moon's movements   14

Going through phases   16

Lunar eclipses   18

Blocking out the Sun   20

High tide, low tide   22

Exploring the Moon   24

Try these activities   28

Full-moon facts   30

Glossary   31

Index & Acknowledgments   32

Meet the Moon

When you look up at the night sky, do you ever wonder about the Moon—the biggest, brightest object in it? You're not alone! People have always been curious about the Moon. For thousands of years, they made up myths and legends to explain what the Moon is, why it changes shape, and why it appears in different parts of the sky on different nights. Today, we use science to explain these mysteries and many others about the Moon.

What is a moon?

Moons are **natural satellites**. They **orbit**, or travel around, a planet. Earth has only one moon, simply called "the Moon," but there are more than 60 other moons in our solar system. No one knows the exact materials of which our moon is made, but scientists believe that it is mainly rock, minerals, and **basalt**. Basalt is hard, dense, dark volcanic rock.

*The orbit of the Moon around Earth is **elliptical**, or oval. The Moon moves at a speed of 2,300 miles (3 683 km) per hour!*

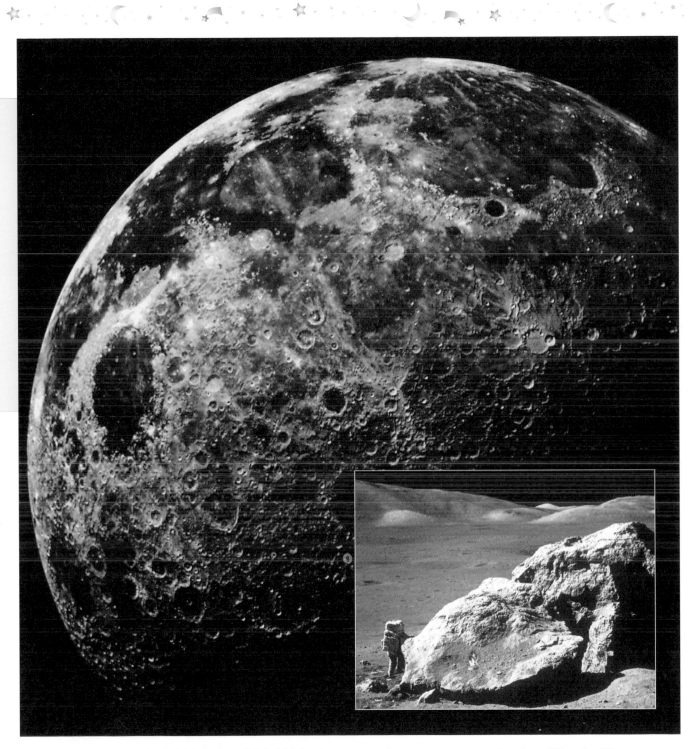

The Moon is about 239,000 miles (384 000 km) from Earth. It is our nearest neighbor in space. The Moon is 2,155 miles (3 468 km) across, or about one-quarter the size of Earth. The smaller photograph shows an American astronaut exploring the surface of the Moon.

How the Moon was "born"

No one knows for certain how the Moon formed. Most scientists believe the Moon was "born" 4 to 5 billion years ago, along with the rest of the solar system. One day, knowing the Moon's beginnings will teach us useful information about how Earth and other bodies in our solar system formed.

There are four main **theories**, or ideas, of how the Moon formed. Scientists came up with the first three before they had the chance to study Moon rocks.

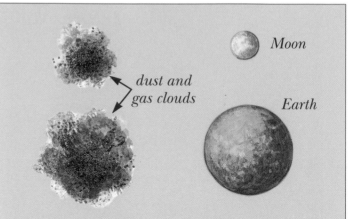

dust and gas clouds

Moon

Earth

1. Solidifying clouds theory
The moons and planets in the solar system formed from clouds of dust and gas that spun very quickly and became tightly packed. Earth and the Moon may have formed from two clouds that were very close together. Once they formed, Earth and the Moon were caught in one another's gravity.

bulge in Earth

Moon flung away

separation complete

Earth

Moon

2. The fission theory
When the Earth was young and still forming, it was almost as soft as pudding. It may have been spinning ten times faster than it does today. It spun so fast that part of it started to bulge. The bulge grew so large that it was flung off the Earth. Over time, it hardened and became the Moon.

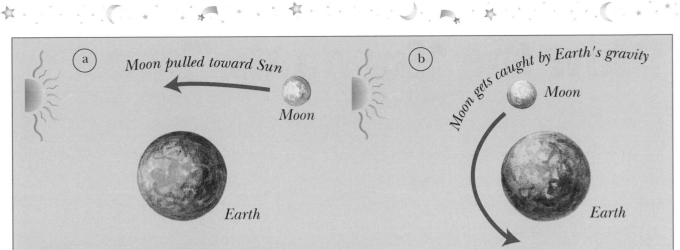

a — Moon pulled toward Sun — Moon — Earth

b — Moon gets caught by Earth's gravity — Moon — Earth

3. The gravitational theory

The Moon may have come from another part of our solar system. It was pulled toward the Sun by the Sun's gravity (a). As it traveled past Earth to the Sun, the Moon was caught by Earth's gravity (b).

Gravity is a force that pulls objects toward one another. All things in space have it. You can read more about gravity on pages 9 and 22.

small planet

These pieces formed the Moon.

Earth

4. The giant impact theory

The newest theory is the **giant impact** theory. Scientists think that when the Earth was young and soft, a small planet crashed into it. Pieces of the Earth's outer layer splashed into space. Many of the pieces joined together and, over time, became the Moon.

The giant impact theory is the one most scientists accept today. After studying Moon rocks, scientists now know that the Moon is made up of materials similar to those in Earth's outer layer. The giant impact theory is the only one that can explain why the Moon is made up of these materials.

What is it like on the Moon?

The Moon is a **dead world**. It has no air or water, and nothing lives there. The Moon does not have an **atmosphere**, as Earth does. An atmosphere is a layer of gases that surrounds a planet or moon. Earth's atmosphere is made up of a few different gases, including nitrogen, oxygen, and carbon dioxide. To stay alive, animals need to breathe oxygen and plants need carbon dioxide.

No sky or sound

During the day, Earth's sky looks like a huge blue dome over our head. Earth's sky is the top layer of the atmosphere. The Moon does not have an atmosphere, so even during the day, the starry blackness of space is overhead. The lack of an atmosphere also makes the Moon a quiet place! Air carries sound. The Moon has no air, so no noise can be heard on the Moon.

This astronaut seems to find the Sun almost unbearably bright, even though he is wearing a thick, dark sun visor!

No sunscreen

Earth's atmosphere acts as a shield that stops many of the Sun's harmful rays from reaching the Earth's surface. It also acts as a blanket, stopping much of the heat from leaving the Earth's surface after the Sun sets. Our atmosphere prevents the Earth from being too hot or cold for living things.

The Moon has no atmosphere, so its surface becomes extremely hot when the Sun is overhead. After the Sun sets, the Moon quickly becomes freezing cold because the day's heat drifts off into space.

Extreme temperatures

When the Sun is directly over the Moon's surface, the temperature soars to 265°F (130°C). When the Sun sets, the temperature falls to -310°F (-190°C).

Lighter loads

Objects have weight because of gravity. The harder it pulls, the more an object weighs. The Moon's gravity is one-sixth as strong as Earth's, so things weigh only one-sixth as much on the Moon. An object that weighs 60 pounds (27 kg) on Earth would weigh only 10 pounds (4.5 kg) on the Moon. Think of all the things you could lift on the Moon!

The lunar landscape

Almost everything on the surface of the Moon is a dull, grayish brown color. A layer of powdery dust or soil covers most of the surface. The dust can be up to 65 feet (20 m) deep! It is made up of tiny pieces of rock. These rock pieces were pounded and crushed by flying space rocks, called **meteorites**, which crashed into the Moon.

Unless a meteorite crashes into it, this footprint could be on the Moon's surface forever. There is no wind to cover it with dust and no rain to wash it away.

Who is the man-in-the-Moon?

Some people think the full moon looks like a face. They call the face the man-in-the-Moon. Long ago, people believed there actually was a man living in the Moon. Today, we know that no one is up there looking down at us. The "face" is the pattern formed by the light and dark areas of the Moon's surface. The bright and shadowy spots are made by the Moon's surface features—mountains, **rilles**, **craters**, and **maria**.

Moon mountains

From Earth, the brightest parts of the Moon are the mountains, or **highlands**. They are the white areas of the man-in-the-Moon. Some mountains are 25,000 feet (7500 m) tall—as tall as the highest mountains on Earth! Scientists believe the mountain chains are the oldest parts of the Moon's surface.

This mountain looks small, but it is actually over 13,000 feet (4 000 m) high! It may look close, but it is more than 18 miles (30 km) from the astronaut who photographed it.

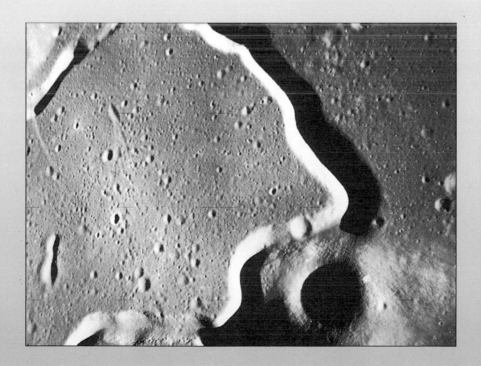

Rilles

The line of light and shadow, shown left, is a channel called a rille. This rille is curved, but some are straight. People once thought rilles were formed by water on the Moon. They believed rilles were made by flowing water because they resemble the riverbeds we have on Earth. Scientists now think **lava** formed the rilles. Lava is hot, melted rock.

Craters and maria

The most famous parts of the Moon's surface are the holes, called **craters**, and dark areas called **maria**. The Moon has hundreds of thousands of craters. Some are only the width of a pinhead. Others are huge. The South Pole Aitken crater may be the biggest crater, not just on the Moon, but in the entire solar system! It is 1,553 miles (2500 km) across. Scientists think most of the larger craters were formed millions to billions of years ago.

Maria

The darkest parts of the lunar landscape are lava-filled craters called maria. They cover more of the Moon's surface than any other feature. Maria were formed when huge meteorites crashed into the Moon so hard that they not only made craters, but they also cracked the rocky surface. Lava oozed out of the cracks and filled the craters. It slowly cooled and hardened into dark rock.

meteor

impact crater

Crash!

Impact craters were formed when meteorites **impacted**, or crashed into, the Moon. The meteorites hit with such speed and force that they dented the surface. The **friction**, or rubbing, of the meteorites against the surface made them so hot that they burned up, leaving behind an empty crater.

Many large impact craters have small mountains in their center. The great heat created by the meteorite rubbing against the Moon's surface melted the rock beneath the meteorite, causing it to splash up from the bottom of the crater. Before it could flow back, the melted rock cooled in the form of a mountain.

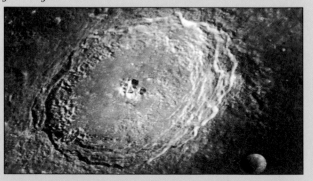

Named by mistake

In 1610, an Italian astronomer named Galileo Galilei looked at the Moon's surface through a homemade telescope. He noticed dark areas that looked as smooth as giant puddles. He mistakenly believed he was looking at seas of water. Galileo named them "maria," which is Latin for "seas." These features are still called maria. In 1998, frozen water was discovered on the Moon, but the maria have no water in them.

The dark, smooth patch near the Moon's horizon is a **mare***, or sea. No one knows why, but one side of the Moon has many maria, and the other has almost none.*

Blown out

Not all craters were formed by impact. Some smaller craters may be **volcanic craters**. These diagrams show how they may have formed.

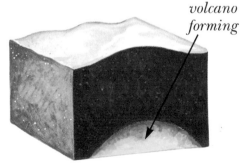

volcano forming

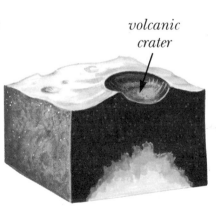

volcanic crater

1. Volcanic action moved gases and melted rock from inside the Moon to its surface.

*2. The gas and rock **erupted**, or burst through the surface of the Moon.*

3. The surface sank into the space left by the eruption, forming a crater.

The Moon's movements

Like all the moons and planets in the solar system, the Moon is a busy body. It is always in motion. The Moon moves in two ways. It **revolves** around, or orbits, the Earth, as the illustration on page 5 shows. It takes about 27 days to make the complete trip. While it is orbiting Earth, the Moon also **rotates**, or spins like a top. The Moon takes 27 days to rotate once. The Earth also rotates, but it only takes 24 hours to spin once.

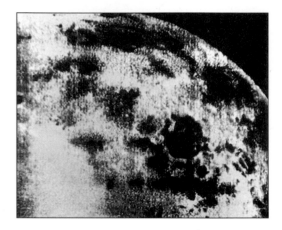

We always see the same side of the Moon from Earth. No one had ever seen the other side until the Luna 3 space probe flew around the Moon and took this picture in 1959.

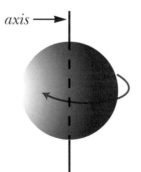

axis →

As a moon or planet rotates, one half of it moves from day to night and the other from night to day. The length of the day and night depends on how fast the moon or planet turns.

A long day

The Moon rotates much more slowly than the Earth, so its days and nights are longer. Since it takes Earth 24 hours to rotate once, each half of the planet gets about 12 hours of daylight and 12 hours of darkness. On the Moon, the Sun is in the sky for almost two Earth weeks before it sets! The sunset is followed by almost two Earth weeks of total darkness.

Near side, far side

Even though the Moon spins, we always see the same side of it from Earth. This side is called the **near side** (marked with the "x"). The side we never see is called the **far side**. We always see the near side because the Moon turns slowly as it moves around Earth. This diagram shows how the Moon spins as it revolves.

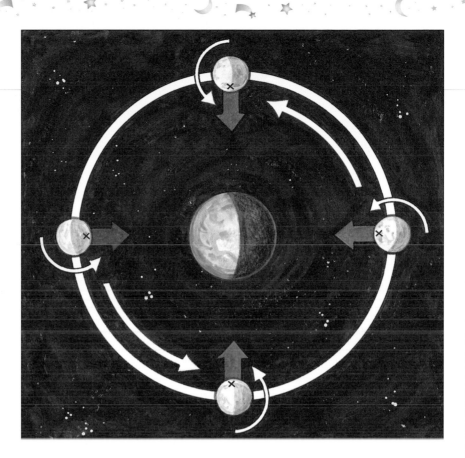

Watch how the Moon moves

This activity will help you see how the Moon rotates as it orbits Earth. You need two paper plates. Using a ruler, find the center of one paper plate and draw a line to the edge.

This plate will be the Moon, and the line will show which is the near side. Poke the pen through the center of the Moon. The pen is the axis. The other paper plate will be Earth.

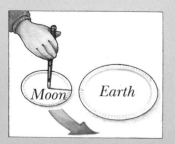
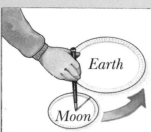

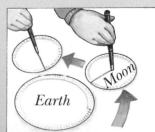

Move the Moon slowly around Earth, making sure that the near-side line always points toward Earth.

Can you understand why we never see the Moon's far side?

Going through phases

The Moon may be bright in our night sky, but it does not make its own light. Moonlight is simply sunlight that has been **reflected**, or bounced, off the Moon's surface. The Moon does not make light or heat the way a star does because it is mainly made of rock. Stars, such as the Sun, are made up of burning gases.

The Moon is like a giant reflector. We do not see it unless sunlight bounces off it.

From far out in space, the Moon always looks the same, as shown by this inner circle of Moons.

The outer circle of Moons shows the sunlit surface we see from Earth.

Earth

Changing shapes

During each month, the Moon seems to change shape several times. The Moon does not actually change, however. As it revolves, our view of it changes, and we can see different parts of its sunlit surface. The amount of Moon that we see is called a **phase**.

The Moon continually changes its position with Earth and the Sun. From Earth, we see different amounts of its lit surface, depending on where the Moon is in its orbit. To better understand phases, try the activity on pages 28-29.

*The lunar cycle starts with the dark **new moon**. Its sunlit side is facing away from Earth.*

*A small **crescent** moon is seen next. As the Moon grows larger, it is described as **waxing**.*

*We see a half-moon at the **first-quarter** phase. The Moon has traveled one-quarter of its orbit.*

*The Moon is now a **waning crescent**. It is only a few days away from becoming a new moon again.*

The lunar month

In ancient times, people watched the phases of the Moon to keep track of time. They made a **lunar calendar** based on the changes of the Moon. It took one lunar month for the Moon to move through its phases and begin the cycle again. The word "month" comes from the word "moon."

*After the first-quarter phase, the Moon is called **gibbous**, which means "humpbacked." Can you guess why?*

*The Moon has traveled three-quarters of its orbit at the **third-quarter** phase.*

*The lit surface **wanes**, or grows smaller. The Moon is described as **waning gibbous**.*

*There is a **full moon** 14 days after the new moon. People say odd things happen at this time.*

Lunar eclipses

When the Sun shines on objects in space, they cast shadows just as things do on Earth. Most of the time, we do not notice Earth's shadow because it falls on empty space. Once in awhile, however, the Moon moves into Earth's shadow. We see the shadow darken the Moon, and a **lunar eclipse** happens. There are about two or three lunar eclipses each year. They last up to four hours. The diagram on the right shows how a lunar eclipse happens.

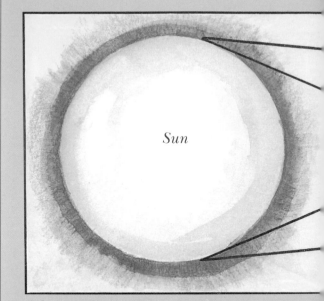

A lunar eclipse can be seen on a clear night by people living on half of the Earth. In this diagram, people on the dark side of Earth can see the eclipse.

Sun

Sun   *Earth*   *Moon*

Tilted trip

Even though the Moon moves around the Earth each month, lunar eclipses do not happen monthly. The Moon's path around Earth is slightly tilted. The Moon, Earth, and Sun do not always line up directly, so the Moon does not always travel through Earth's shadow and cause an eclipse. It usually passes a little above or below Earth's shadow.

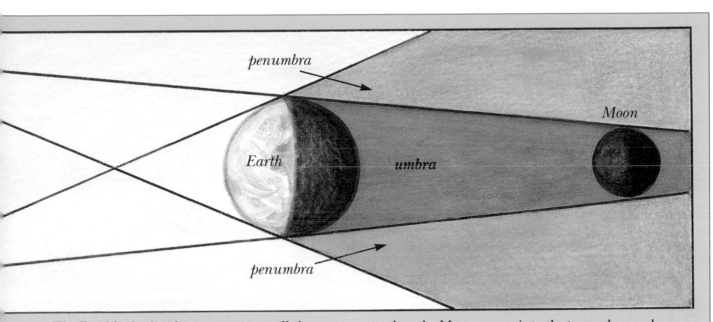

*The Earth's shadow has gray parts, called **penumbras**, and a dark part, called the **umbra**. The umbra is a double shadow created when the penumbras overlap one another. An eclipse begins when the Moon moves into the penumbra and dims a little. As it moves into the darker umbra, it dims much more. After a few hours, it moves out of the umbra and passes into the penumbra again.*

Big Red

During a lunar eclipse, the Moon grows dim, and its bright surface glows a dark orangy red. The Moon itself does not change color, however. It appears red to us on Earth because of the way sunlight reaches it. During an eclipse, the Earth is between the Sun and Moon, so sunlight must pass through the Earth's atmosphere. The atmosphere bends the sunlight, separating it into different colors—red, orange, yellow, green, blue, indigo, and violet. The red light is the only one that can reach the Moon. It bounces off the Moon's surface, making the Moon appear red.

Blocking out the Sun

During a **solar eclipse**, the Moon moves between the Earth and the Sun, as shown in the diagram on the right. The Moon casts a shadow on part of the Earth. There are three types of solar eclipses—**partial**, **total**, and **annular**.

The Sun is 400 times the size of the Moon. How can the Moon block it from our view? During a total eclipse, the Moon is exactly 400 times closer to Earth than the Sun is to Earth. From Earth, the Sun and Moon appear to be the same size.

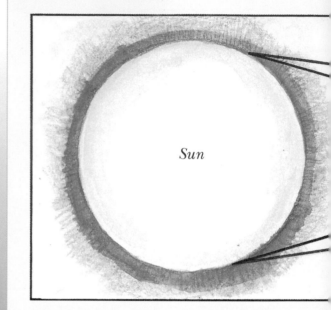

Sun

Warning: *Never look at a solar eclipse! Looking at one can damage your eyes permanently.*

how the Sun appears from Earth during a total eclipse

the Sun during an annular eclipse

the Sun in a partial eclipse

These pictures show the three types of solar eclipses. Look at where the dark and light parts of the Moon's shadow fall. How do the shadows differ in each type of eclipse?

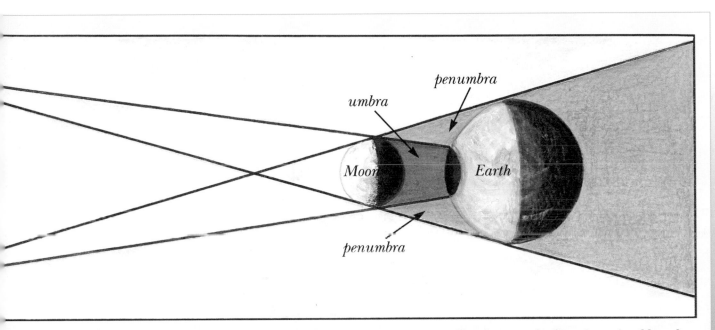

A total solar eclipse happens in the area where the umbra falls. There are one or two total eclipses each year, but they are not always noticeable. From *any spot on Earth, a total eclipse is noticeable only once every 360 years! A partial eclipse happens in the area where the penumbra falls.*

Annular eclipse

The Moon's orbit around Earth is not a perfect circle. It is elliptical (turn back to page 4 to see the Moon's orbit). If its orbit were circular, the Moon would always be the same distance from Earth. Its oval orbit takes the Moon farther from Earth at some times than at others. An **annular eclipse** happens when the Moon is at a distant point in its orbit. During an annular eclipse, the Moon is farther from the Earth than during a total eclipse, so it cannot completely block the Sun. We can see the edge of the Sun around the Moon.

In this annular eclipse, the Moon has not yet moved all the way in front of the Sun.

High tide, low tide

Gravity is a force found everywhere in the universe. It **attracts**, or pulls, objects toward one another. Earth's gravity pulls things toward the center of the planet. The saying "whatever goes up must come down" is a good way to describe how we experience gravity on Earth. If we jump up, Earth's gravity always pulls us down. It not only keeps our feet on the ground—it also holds the Moon in its orbit around Earth.

*Water levels rise and fall every day. The different water levels are called high and low **tides**.*

Attracted to the Moon

Everything in space has gravity. The Moon's gravity is weaker than Earth's, but it is strong enough to affect our planet. In fact, the Moon affects Earth more than any of the other moons in our solar system affect their planets. As the Moon moves around Earth, its gravity pulls the water in our oceans and lakes and causes tides.

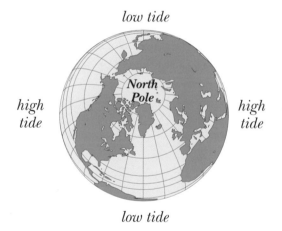

When it is high tide on one side of Earth, it is always high tide on the side directly across from it. When it is low tide on one side of the world, it is always low tide on the other side. The pattern of tides shown above follows the Moon as it travels around Earth, which is why every shore in the world has high and low tides.

There are two high and low tides every day on every beach in the world. After a high tide, it takes about six hours for the water to fall to a low-tide level. High tides are 12 hours, 25 ½ minutes apart. Look at these two pictures. How can you tell that it is high tide in the top picture and low tide in the one on the bottom? Name five things that have changed from high tide to low tide.

Exploring the Moon

For thousands of years, people have dreamed of reaching the Moon. In the 1950s and 1960s, the United States' space agency, called **NASA**, and the former Soviet Union launched spacecraft that helped make this dream come true. These scientific spacecraft carried **probes**, which gathered information about the Moon. Some of the information gathered by the probes helped scientists prepare to land astronauts on the Moon.

Spacecraft to the Moon

• In January, 1959, the Soviet *Luna 1* became the first spacecraft to fly past the Moon.

• In 1959, *Luna 2* became the first probe to crash onto the Moon.

• In 1959, *Luna 3* took the first photographs of the far side.

• Between 1964 and 1968, NASA launched the Ranger, Surveyor, and Lunar Orbiter probes to take close-up images of the Moon.

• In 1970, *Luna 16* returned to Earth with the first samples of Moon dust ever collected.

• In 1994, the U.S. Department of Defense's Clementine probe indicated that there might be ice on the Moon. Scientists think that comets might have left the ice billions of years ago.

Surveyor probes such as the one on the left landed softly on the Moon. Before these probes landed, scientists were not sure that a craft could make a landing without disappearing into the Moon dust.

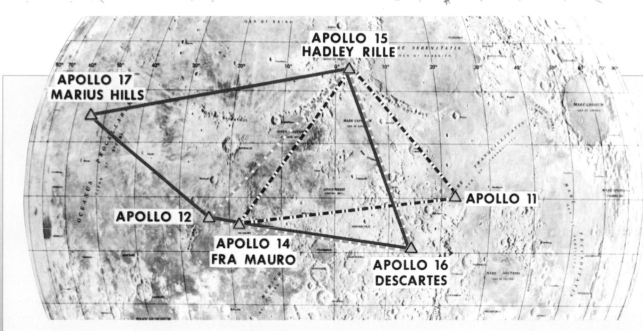

APOLLO 15
HADLEY RILLE

APOLLO 17
MARIUS HILLS

APOLLO 12

APOLLO 14
FRA MAURO

APOLLO 16
DESCARTES

APOLLO 11

Mapping the Moon

All of NASA's probes took close-up pictures of the Moon's surface. Scientists pieced together the images to make a map. They also used them to find the most interesting landing sites for astronauts. The map above shows the sites where astronauts landed. The program that sent people to the Moon was called Apollo.

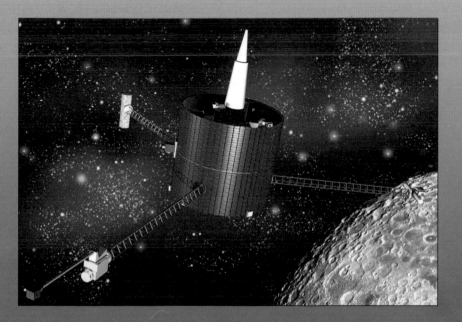

Looking for answers

In 1998, NASA launched Lunar Prospector to learn more about the Moon. The probe's mission is to collect information about the composition of the Moon, which will help scientists find out how the Moon formed. Since its launch, Lunar Prospector has shown that there really is ice at the poles of the Moon, as the Clementine probe's findings suggested.

The Eagle has landed

On July 20, 1969, the dream of reaching the Moon came true. Two American astronauts aboard a small spacecraft called the Eagle headed toward the Moon's surface. People around the world watched the trip on television, holding their breath until one of the astronauts announced, "The Eagle has landed." Humans were finally on the Moon!

Neil Armstrong photographed Buzz Aldrin as he climbed from the Eagle.

One small step...

Neil Armstrong, one of the astronauts aboard the Eagle, became the first person ever to step on the Moon. As he climbed from the spacecraft and placed his foot on the dusty lunar surface, he said the famous words, "That's one small step for a man, one giant leap for mankind." Armstrong and the other astronaut, Buzz Aldrin, spent just over two hours on the Moon. After this first visit, astronauts made five more trips to the Moon. Since 1972, no one has been on the Moon.

(above) Armstrong and Aldrin left this plaque on the Moon.

(right) It was difficult for the astronauts to move in their stiff, bulky suits. On the last few missions, the **lunar rover** made it easier to get around.

Working on the Moon

Apollo astronauts did not just walk around on the Moon. They set up scientific equipment and experiments. They also collected 842 pounds (382 kg) of Moon rocks for scientists to study. The astronauts had to wear special suits on the Moon. The suits protected them from the Sun's heat and dangerous rays from space. They also provided air pressure to keep the astronauts' blood from boiling. The astronauts carried oxygen tanks so they could breathe.

Try these activities

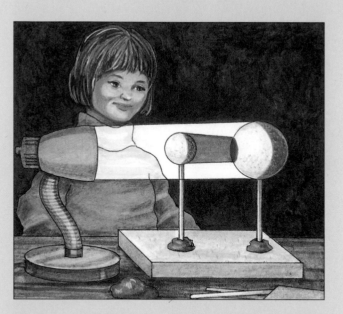

Make a lunar and solar eclipse

You will need 2 styrofoam® balls, 2 straws, plasticine, a box lid, a desk lamp, and a ruler.

Set up the lamp at one end but do not turn it on. Roll 2 balls of plasticine and press them onto the box lid so that they line up with the lamp, as shown above. Push one end of a straw into the center of each styrofoam® ball and the other end into a plasticine base. You can make a solar or a lunar eclipse, depending on which ball you place closer to the lamp. The smaller ball (Moon) closer to the lamp will create a solar eclipse; the larger ball (Earth) closer will make a lunar eclipse. Turn on the lamp and turn out the other lights in the room. What has happened to the ball that is farthest from the lamp?

Phases

Try this experiment to show the phases of the Moon.

You need a bright desk lamp and a large ball. Angle the lamp so that the light is shining straight out to one side. Stand facing the light, holding the ball out in front of you. Hold it slightly higher than your face. How does the ball look? It is dark, like the new moon, because the lamp is shining on its far side.

Moon base

Many people believe that, in the next century, humans will build a base on the Moon. Draw a picture of how you think the Moon base might look. Remember some of the things you have learned about the Moon and what it is like to be on its surface (turn back to pages 8-9 and 26-27 if you need help). Here are some questions to ask yourself:

How will people breathe?
Where will they get food and water?
How will they prepare their meals?
How will bathrooms work?
What will people do for fun?

Turn slowly, making sure your head does not block the lamp's light. Watch as the lit part of the ball grows larger and then smaller.

Do you recognize the phases of the Moon that were shown on page 9? Name the phases as you see them appear on the ball.

When your picture is finished, build a model of your Moon base. Make a list of materials you will need. Here are some ideas for building materials:

construction paper
cardboard boxes
paper tubes
aluminum foil
pipe cleaners
scissors, tape, and glue
paints and markers

When your Moon base is finished, offer your friends or family a tour and explain how everything works!

Full-moon facts

Read the four fun facts on this page, and next time there's a full moon, you can use the information to impress your friends.

The "shrinking" Moon

Have you ever noticed that a full moon looks larger when it is near the horizon, as above, than when it is high in the sky? This difference in size is an **optical illusion**—your eyes are playing tricks on you. Scientists believe the Moon may look larger near the horizon because it is closer to things we can compare it to, such as buildings and trees.

*When the Moon is a waning crescent, we sometimes see "the old moon in the arms of the new," above. Even though the Moon is not full, we see all of it because of **earthshine**. Earthshine is sunlight that bounces off the Earth's surface. It is not as bright as sunlight, which is why the part of the Moon it lights is dim compared to the sunlit crescent.*

There is usually only one full moon each month, but every two-and-a-half years, there are two full moons in a month. The second one is called a **blue moon**. Can you guess what "once in a blue moon" means? It describes something that does not happen often.

The full moon of each month has its own name

January	wolf moon
February	snow moon
March	worm moon
April	pine moon
May	flower moon
June	strawberry moon
July	buck moon
August	corn moon
September	harvest moon
October	hunter's moon
November	beaver moon
December	cold moon

Glossary

astronaut A person who has been trained to fly aboard spacecraft

atmosphere The gases that surround a planet

basalt Hard, dense, dark volcanic rock

crater A hole in the Moon's surface

eclipse The darkening of the Sun or Moon when light coming from the Sun is blocked

ellipse An oval shape

fission The splitting of the nucleus, or center, of an atom

friction The rubbing of one object or surface against another

gibbous The phase of the Moon when more than its half is illuminated

gravity The force that pulls people toward the center of a planet or moon

lava Hot, melted rock that reaches the Earth's surface through a crack or volcano

lunar rover A vehicle designed to carry two people on the surface of the Moon

maria The Latin word for seas; dark craters on the Moon's surface that were once thought to be water

meteorite A chunk of stone or metallic matter that has fallen to Earth from space

NASA National Aeronautics and Space Administration; the agency in charge of the U.S. exploration of space

optical illusion An image that fools the eye into believing it is real

orbit (n) The path taken by a natural or artificial satellite in space; (v) to travel around a planet or star

phase A stage of development

penumbra The lighter, outer edge of Earth's shadow

probe A robot carried into space by a scientific spacecraft that sends back information about moons, planets, and other objects in the solar system

reflect To throw back light rays, heat, or sounds that strike a surface; the Moon reflects the Sun's rays

revolve To turn

rille A groove on the Moon's surface that scientists believe was formed by lava

rotate To spin

satellite A natural or artificial object that travels around a planet or moon

solar system The Sun, all the planets, their moons, and other heavenly bodies that orbit the Sun

theory A guess or judgment made to explain why something happens

tide The change in the level of water in the oceans and seas on Earth, caused by the gravity of the Sun and Moon

umbra The completely dark part of a shadow cast by the Earth or Moon during an eclipse

waning To decrease, or seem to decrease in size, as the Moon does when it passes from full Moon to new Moon

waxing To grow, or seem to grow larger, as the Moon does when it passes from new moon to full moon

Index

activities 15, 28-29
Aldrin, Buzz 26, 27
Apollo 25
Armstrong, Neil 26, 27
astronauts 8, 11, 24, 25, 26, 27
atmosphere 8, 19
birth of Moon 6-7
craters 10, 12-13
Eagle, the 26
eclipses 18-21, 28
exploration 24-25
far side 14, 15, 24
full-moon facts 30
Galileo 13
gases 8, 13, 16
gravity 6, 7, 9, 22
landscape 10-11
lava 11, 12, 13

lunar calendar 17
lunar eclipse 18-19
Lunar Prospector 25
lunar rover 27
man-in-the-Moon 10, 11
map of Moon 25
maria 10, 12-13
meteorites 10, 12
Moon dust 10, 24
Moon rocks 6, 7, 16, 27
moonlight 16
moons 4, 5
mountains 10, 11, 12
movements of Moon 14-15
NASA 24, 25
near side 15
orbit 4, 5, 14, 15, 16, 17, 18, 21, 22
phases 16-17, 28, 29

planets 5, 7, 8, 14, 22
rilles 10, 11
rotation 14
satellite 4, 5
size 5
solar eclipse 20-21
solar system 4, 5, 6, 7, 12, 14, 22
space probes 14, 24, 25
space suits 27
spacecraft 24, 26
Sun 8, 9, 14, 16, 18, 19, 20, 27
sunlight 16, 19, 30
surface 9, 10-11, 12-13, 16, 25, 26
temperatures 8, 9
tides 22-23
volcanic action 13
water 11, 13, 22, 24
working on Moon 27

Acknowledgments

Photographs
Chris Crumley/Earth Water: page 23 (both)
NASA: pages 8, 11 (bottom), 12, 13, 26 (top),
    27 (top left)
NASA/Ames Research Center: page 25
Photo Researchers, Inc.:
    Larry Landolfi: page 30 (left)
    David Nunuk/Science Photo Library: title page
    NASA/Science Photo Library: pages 11 (top),
        26-27
    John Sanford/Science Photo Library: page 19
    Science Photo Library: page 14

Photo Researchers, Inc., continued:
    Pekka Parviainen/Science Photo Library:
        page 30 (right)
Photri, Inc.: page 24
Photri, Inc./NASA: page 25 (top)
Other photographs by Digital Stock and
    Digital Vision

Illustrations
All illustrations by Barbara Bedell except
    the following: Mike Campeau: page 9

1 2 3 4 5 6 7 8 9 0   Printed in the U.S.A.   7 6 5 4 3 2 1 0 9 8